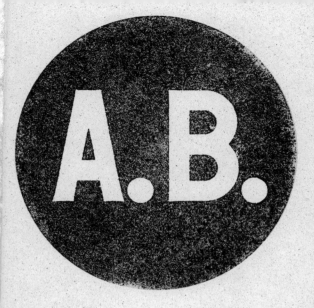

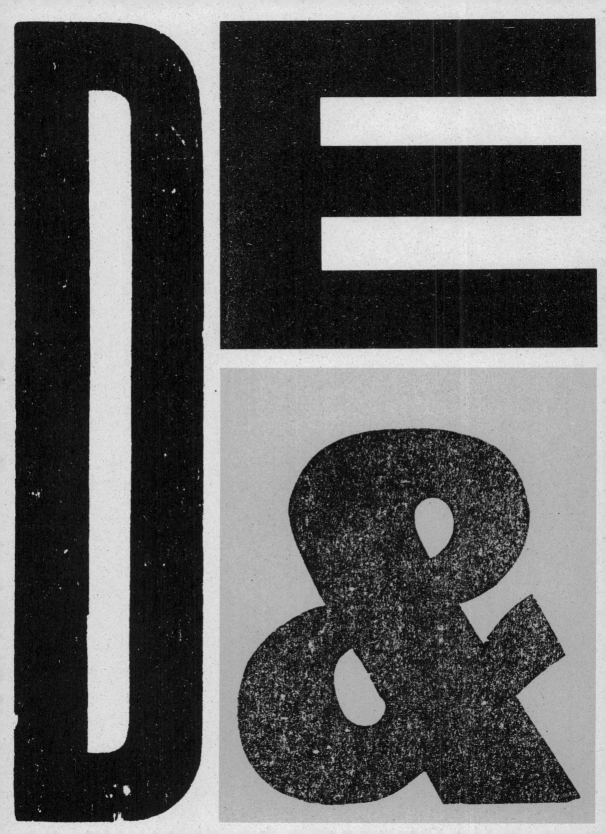

I've always been an avid collector of printed ephemera and interesting pieces of found type, it's a huge source of inspiration for me. Wherever I go I've always picked up tickets, scraps of type, newspaper clippings, odd packaging and anything that caught my eye that I thought could be useful for inspiration.

Lots of the material I've collected is now over 20 years old, it's got an interesting quality, there's a pre-digital feel to the material. It's from a time when things were still made by hand, I like the individuality of it.

For Peter Dougherty

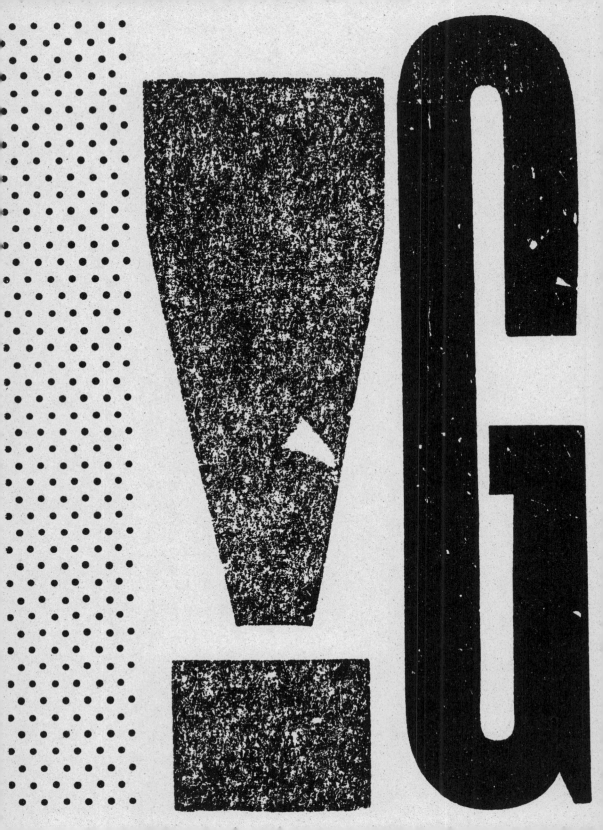

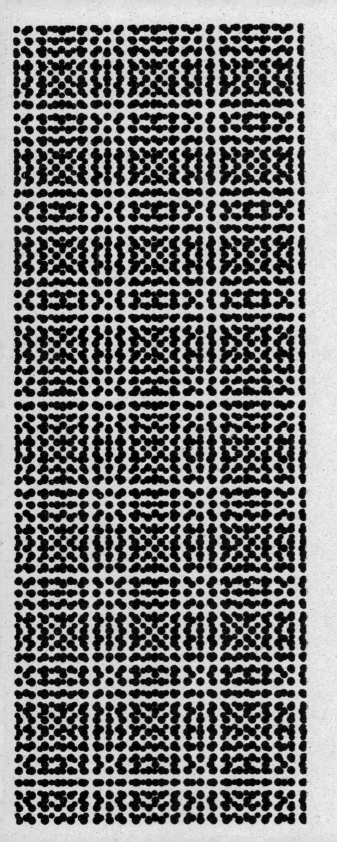

MAKE IT NOW!

GO EVERY WHERE DO EVERY THING

My grandfather, Harry Wardle, influenced me hugely in the way I live my life. He was a natural storyteller and fired my imagination and thirst for knowledge. He taught me to be continually positive, always inquisitive and eager to seek out new experiences. These are the qualities that I believe are the key to creativity.

As a boy, I was my grandfather's travelling companion and partner in crime. We went to Italy, North Africa, Greece, Turkey, Russia, Hong Kong and China. Every day on these trips was spent visiting historic sites, museums, art galleries and eating exotic food. In the evenings my grandfather would read and I would fill scrapbooks with leaflets, tickets and bits of ephemera I'd picked up during the day. That early introduction to collecting ephemera, making sketchbooks and sharing my ideas and experiences with others sparked a creative urge that has never left me.

Polaroid photographs taken on a trip to China in 1981. Soaking up new influences is an important part of forming your creative DNA.

Collecting printed ephemera has
provided me with lots of inspiration,
nothing beats the smell of ink on paper.

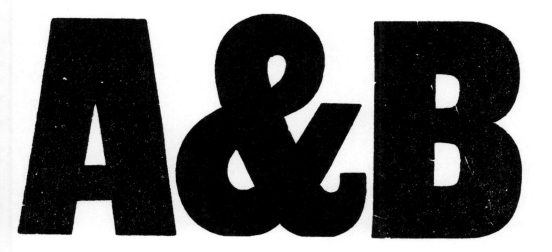

As a teenager I was obsessed with everything to do with music; the sleeves, logos and promo videos all fascinated me. I grew up in the 1980s, a decade when the visual image in pop had become as important as the music. My favourite bands of the time – The Human League, Kraftwerk, Japan, Adam and the Ants – each had an incredibly distinct image. I would spend hours in my bedroom studying the record sleeves and listening to the music.

My absolute favourite of these was The Human League. They were different from everything else going on in music; weird, quirky, artistic and they wrote catchy pop songs. The first record I bought by them was 'Being Boiled', a truly weird-sounding song concerned with silk-production methods – not an obvious subject for a three-minute pop song! It was the peculiar oddness of their image and music that drew me to the band. The haircuts, clothes, analogue synthesisers and drum machines made them seem impossibly cool. I listened intently to the music and studied the extraordinary sleeve design.

This was my first memorable experience of design and music coming together to make something that really excited me and fired my imagination. It showed me what design is and what it's capable of being. Design was a doorway to something new for me; I realised that design is everywhere as a tool of communication. For me, design is art with purpose.

A.B.

Luckily my initials are the first two
letters of the alphabet, I was born
to be a graphic designer.

I had a summer job at a printer's owned by a friend of my father. It was a small place, producing all kinds of print for local businesses. They also printed letterpress beer mats, and that was what really fascinated me. It was the first time I'd seen the letterpress process and at the time I thought it was only ever used for making beer mats.

The beer mats were printed in three colours using separate plates. The material being used for the mats was a soft absorbent card, so the print impression had to be quite heavy, giving a slight indent to the finished design. I thought this was great and was intrigued by the process. I can trace my love of letterpress back to those beer mats.

It was while I was working in the printer's that I first saw a graphic designer at work, preparing artwork for the beer mats. Watching the artwork being prepared and then going to press to be printed gave me my first insight into the design and print process; I was intrigued by the methods involved in taking the design from the drawing board, making the plates and then printing the design. By watching these stages I could see how it had been done, step by step. It was something I wanted to learn how to do.

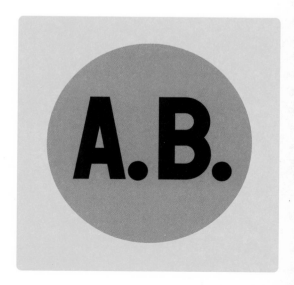

LEARN TO LOOK

I spent three years studying Graphic Design at Leeds Poly. Going to art school is a calling for a particular type of person, for someone who is looking for something different. That was my reason for going to art school, I wanted to explore and find out things. I wasn't a scientist or a mathematician, I knew where my strengths lay and I hoped that art school would be a nurturing environment for me.

My contemporaries at art school weren't too concerned with becoming commercial designers – they were the oddballs of their generation. To me, it felt like a hugely experimental environment where people were finding out about themselves as much as anything else. It was a non-judgemental place that encouraged personal growth and self-discovery. It was a place that encouraged creative play; we were given room to experiment and develop our creative strategies. Without these years of creative development I wouldn't have had the chance to define my approach to design.

It's hard to quantify creative development; it's an organic process and sometimes difficult to explain. It's about developing sensitivity and understanding. Learning a new vocabulary of describing the world and how you see it.

SCHWITTERS

While studying at Leeds I was obsessed with Dada artist Kurt Schwitters, I produced lots of work directly inspired by his collages. This is when I first became interested in combining typography, texture and colour to produce my work.

LEARN TO SEE

After Leeds I found myself at the Royal College of Art, in London. It was a huge cultural shift for me; it was the first time I'd lived away from home and I found myself mixing with people from very different backgrounds. The course was more structured and traditional than what I was used to. I kicked against the teaching, rebelling in my own way.

After two years I graduated with an MA and some really good friends. My view of design had been broadened enormously but I still didn't know how I fitted into the 'real world'. I don't think any of us did, so we started making our own way and pursuing our own agendas.

The work I produced at the RCA was a continuation of the collage experiments I'd been making at Leeds. There was a shift of emphasis from simply mastering technique to making work that communicated a message on the MA course, something that at first I found hard to grasp.

Royal College of Art

Department of

Graphic Art & Design

Beauty

oq of Art

My work was still very experimental at this stage, I was trying to find my own voice and work out what I had to say.

The studio space I shared at the
Royal College of Art. Note the lack
of computers. Contrast this with my
current studio pictured later on.

ANNA LOVES HORSES

As part of my graduation show I showed a short tape slide presentation called 'Anna Loves Horses'. It told the life story of Anna Sewell, the author of *Black Beauty*. It was a very strange little piece – all my friends loved it because it was so weird and odd, the teaching staff were less sure of its merits.

At the show someone came up to me with his business card – it was Peter Dougherty, who was creative director of MTV Europe. He had just set up an office in London and wanted me to come and see him. A couple of weeks later, he gave me my first commission, to design a series of channel idents. Peter loved the fact that I was weird and slightly odd and encouraged me in many ways. He gave me the confidence to set up my own small studio, to work independently and develop my own voice. Being commissioned by MTV was a huge boost for me, it encouraged me to believe in what I was doing and to listen to my instincts.

To make 'Anna Loves Horses' I used photos of my sister taken from family albums. I've always been autobiographical with my work; I think it's important to make work that has an emotional connection.

I met Emma Parker while we were both studying at the Royal College of Art. For me, it was love at first sight; it took me a while to convince her of my charms, but thankfully she came round in the end. Emma was studying photography and her work at college was dreamlike, surreal and beautiful. Once she graduated, Emma's work was in high demand, so I spent the first few years after college as her assistant, working with her on campaigns and exhibitions.

After we were married (by Elvis in Las Vegas) and we had our children, Emma decided to step away from her photography career. We now work together in our studio – she runs the business side of things and comes up with all my best ideas. Of all the people who have shaped my life and career, Emma has been the most influential, she is my harshest critic and knows what I'm trying to say even before I do.

We all need encouragement and reassurance to thrive. It's important to have a strong support network of friends to help you survive in the real world of life after college. It's tough to stay motivated and keep true to your ideals, so if there's someone there to share these times with you, it makes a huge difference.

This photo of Emma and myself
was taken during our honeymoon in
San Francisco, we both appreciate
the surreal nature of the everyday.

I AM HERE!

At the time when I graduated it was really tough to break into the industry; we didn't have the networks that are around now. I was ridiculously shy and I didn't like ringing people up on the phone, so it was hard for me to get my work out there. I started off by making little photocopied books and postcards to send to people, finding ways of producing unique printed material that would stand out. That's how I started printmaking, and it developed into making posters and the kind of work that I do now.

My social awkwardness was the reason why I made the work I did – to avoid having to speak to people on the phone! It's funny how something that initially could be seen as a weakness eventually helps you to define yourself and to stand out from the crowd. You shouldn't feel that you have to be a certain type to succeed, the main thing is to be driven and believe in what you are doing. Be consistent with your message and don't worry too much about trying to fit in.

My photocopy books were showcases of my visual language and my approach to work. I used clip-art and collected ephemera and photocopied type to produce them, it was all cheap and available. I can trace my use of language back to these books.

Sweet Shop is one of the early self-published photocopy books. It's about simple optimism, seeing the world through wide eyes and finding inspiration in unlikely places.

SLOW LANE

THE WORLD IS A GIANT SWEET SHOP

T.V. DINNER

FAST LANE

I didn't have any fancy equipment at the time, I could never imagine owning or learning how to use a computer. By necessity I had to be resourceful, but that turned out to be just what I needed to make my work; there's always a solution to figure out, and that helps you to think creatively.

I would produce around fifty copies of each book and post them out to prospective clients and potential collaborators. They were quirky enough to be noticed; they had a particular look that was consistent over the series. I made them all the same size, each based on six sheets of A3 paper folded to make a twenty-one page book. Some were made from a number of different coloured paper pages and others were black and white. They were short on information; I never really explained what they were for or who they were from. I included contact details, but I never really expected anyone would ever get in touch.

The first person to commission me to produce work as a result of making the photocopy books was Erik Kessels. At the time, my studio set-up was very simple – I had a shoebox containing art materials and a few books of type and pictograms for reference, and I used the photocopier in the local cornershop. Together, Erik and I created the campaign that would really kick things off for me.

I had hardly any money to produce these early pieces, so had to be ingenious and economical. This is something that is still part of me as a designer, I like to say the most using the least.

I've always been fascinated by vernacular typography, hand-painted signs, scrawled messages – work that is simple and direct. But the rules and terminology of typography baffled me initially. It was only when I started using letterforms as part of my collage work that I began to understand it.

Typography seemed to be about small point sizes, laying out text and legibility. At the time I was looking at how pop artists from the sixties had used type. Artists like Jasper Johns, Robert Indiana and Ed Ruscha used type in such an inspiring way, using the letterforms as abstract elements in their compositions.

The only way that I had of working with type was to photocopy fonts from specimen books. Then cutting out individual letters and hand-positioning them, laboriously glueing down each letter to make words and layouts. This handmade technique had a huge impact on how my work looked. When I enlarged type the photocopier gave it a rough texture that I liked. It seemed to make the type come to life, giving

This font was sent to me by my friend Tim who was teaching in Jamaica. He'd found an old print shop there and printed a set of typographic posters.

I love the textured look and feel of the type, something that is impossible to achieve any other way.

ABCDEFGHI
JKLMNOPQR
STUVWXYZ
12345
67890

the letterforms a rough feel that felt spontaneous. I quickly became expert at using the photocopier, enlarging and reducing type and incorporating found ephemera and clip-art. This gave my work a simple quality; because I had limited options, I had to be resourceful.

I collected type specimen books to expand my choice of letterforms and gradually built up a small library of fonts. I collected metal stencil letters, tracing their shapes to produce usable fonts. I bought full fonts of stickers from hardware shops and photocopied them. I liked to hunt down odd fonts that weren't in any graphic-design manuals. I draw a lot of inspiration from 'folk typography', work produced by non-designers. I like simple type with enough character to feel individual.

Typography is very hard to get right – I'm still learning how to do it. Good typography is hard to teach, it's something you have to work on constantly.

Later, I developed a way of working using letterpress and I've now worked with wood type for over ten years. I'm interested in it for the quality of print and the feeling of restriction, the limitations of the process and the impact it has on the design and layout of the posters. I think it helps me to produce ingenious work. A lot of my early projects had small budgets, so I had to be clever with print in order to make interesting work. I like to work within boundaries.

There is an endless variety in letterforms, there is always something new to be inspired by. My collection of stencils, stickers and signs provides me with huge inspiration.

SEE THE COLOUR

I also apply the same thinking to how I use colour. When to use it and how to use it effectively is a key part of my work. I find it easier to work with a reduced colour palette, to limit the options I have and to keep it simple – yellow, blue, red and black.

I like to use colours undiluted and as pure as possible. If I'm going to use yellow, I'll use the brightest, clearest version of yellow I can find. I specify pure colour to print with – bright red, clear yellow and strong green, colour straight out of the tin!

My local screen printer, Harvey Lloyd, has a shelf of tins with my favourite colours. We've named them 'A.B. Red', 'A.B. Yellow', etc. It makes things easier and this way I can guarantee consistency across projects.

I love black and white as much as I love colour. I like to reduce the visual information as much as possible, to keep the visual simple and clear and concentrate on the message I'm trying to convey. I try to be adventurous with colour and go through cycles trying particular combinations and effects, then moving on to a new variation to keep things fresh.

Choosing the right words to use is important, avoid cliché and well worn phrases. Look for unexpected poetry and meaning in the everyday.

THE SUN SHINES HERE EVERY DAY!

My experience growing up and at art school, from my first commissions to my best work, through the people I've met and the relationships I've made, have all influenced the way I live, the work I produce and how I work. Everyone is different and will have different ways of going about things, these are a few of my thoughts on creativity and getting things done, and I hope you find them useful. I hope this book will inspire and encourage you. If you're stuck for an idea, have a big decision to handle or need a new perspective on a problem, here are some approaches for thinking, communicating and creativity. An upbeat guide that anyone can use to help with the big and small challenges we face every day.

The phrases in my work have all got a few things in common, there's always an element of humour, a lightness of touch – they don't take life or the world too seriously. They surprise or provoke, in a playful way, making you think or look at something a bit differently – and they speak truth, I try to keep it honest in everything I do. Humour, provocation and truth are a powerful combination if you want to communicate your ideas successfully. I hope these prints speak to you and you can take something useful from them.

There are a good few pieces of advice in this book, but if I could only offer you one, this wouldn't be a bad one. It's my most popular print and resonates with lots of different people in different ways. Work by it, live by it and you can't go far wrong:

I made this poster in 2004; it's since gone on to become my best-known piece of work. It's hard to keep things simple, by concentrating on the words with a simple design the message is made clear.

WORK HARD

&

BE NICE TO PEOPLE

Being inquisitive is the key to creativity

I LIKE IT. WHAT IS IT?

YOU ARE HERE!

Find the extraordinary in the ordinary.

Being in a new environment forces you to question yourself about everything.

Changing your daily routine makes you look at the world through fresh eyes.

You can discover more in the first day somewhere new than in a week at home.

Document everything, take photographs, collect things and keep mementoes.

Seeing the world helps you to put you and your work in context.

I'm constantly looking out for examples of interesting typefaces and graphic images. Seeing new things helps to spark off new ideas.

CUT IT OUT

The collage technique is a great model that can be applied to all creative thinking and making. You can use this technique to loosen up your thoughts. Combine images and words in your head to help develop original ideas.

The solution to a problem can be found in its individual parts. There is always a way of pulling apart a problem to find out how to put it back together in a new and interesting way. The palette of methods, materials and ideas you accumulate is what makes up your DNA as a designer. We draw on this to create each new piece of work.

My creative roots are in collage, it's a technique I've always been drawn to and interested in. I respond to the inherent restrictions of collage, I like only being able to make something with what I have to hand.

Combining colour, texture and scale is important when making a composition. Develop your layout skills by using collages; gather together material from different sources and combine it to make new work.

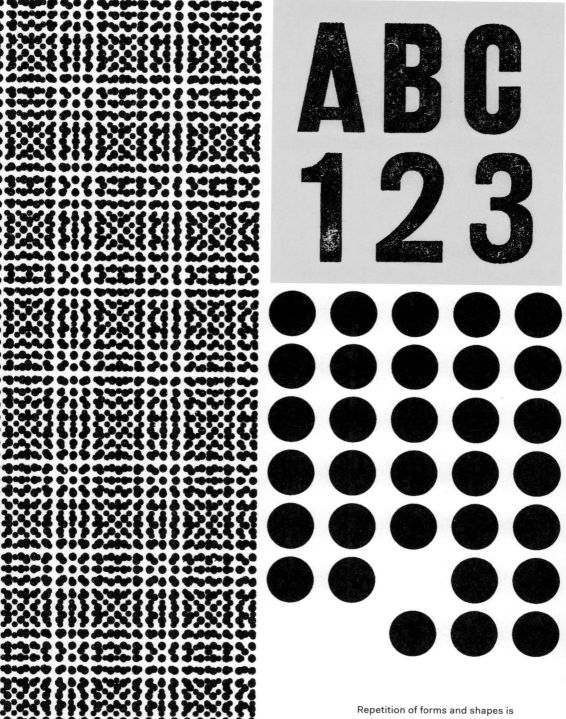

Repetition of forms and shapes is
one of my favourite techniques, I like
making patterns and combining it with
type. Here I've used a simple grid to
gather interesting patterns and shapes
to create a satisfying composition.

ALL YOU NEED TO KNOW ABOUT GRAPHIC DESIGN

When I was on my Art Foundation course I went to a presentation from a Letraset salesman and was given a copy of their catalogue and a poster of typefaces. I was fascinated by it; all the different fonts, clip art and patterns were listed in the book. It was everything I needed to know about graphic design.

I didn't realise it at the time, but this was going to be hugely influential for me as a designer. I've still got the book on my shelf, it's battered and torn after twenty-five years of use. It feels like it's from a different age now – the Letraset system was based on a dry transfer method of setting type. You would buy individual sheets of letters and use them to set type by rubbing down each letter individually, kerning would be done by eye, guided by small lines on the printed sheet. It was very difficult to do and often resulted in irregular letter spacing, cracked characters and wobbly lines of type. At least it did in my hands.

Whilst I was leafing through the catalogue I came across a page of line illustrations featuring groovy 1970s-looking people depicted in various glamorous scenarios. Then I noticed a particularly familiar couple cheerily dancing, they were the same people I'd seen on the front cover of 'Being Boiled' by The Human League. I looked further and identified the fonts that had also been used (Eurostyle and Peignot, if you're interested!). This was a revelation for me, now I knew where this stuff came from. This was how to be a graphic designer!

Design is everywhere and in everything. Keep your eyes and mind open. Investigate and respond to what you're drawn to.

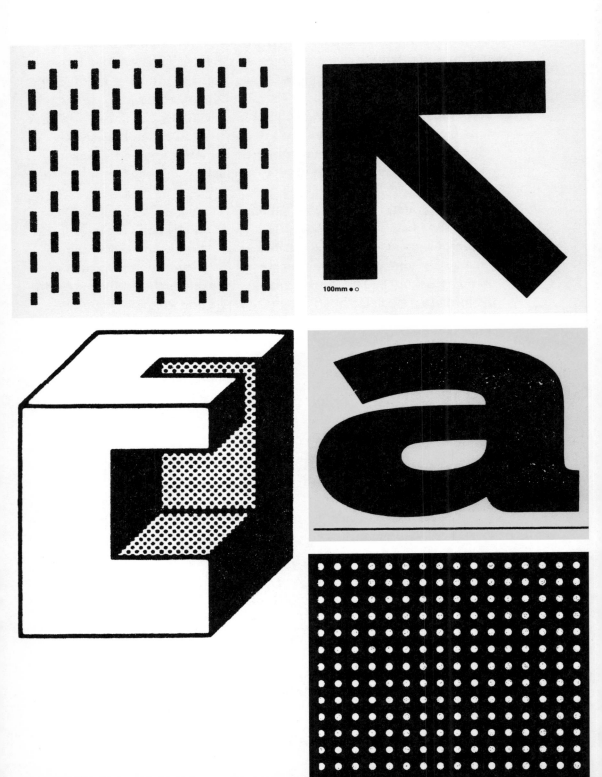

100mm ● ○

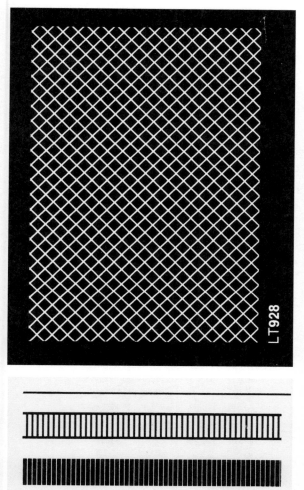

LT928

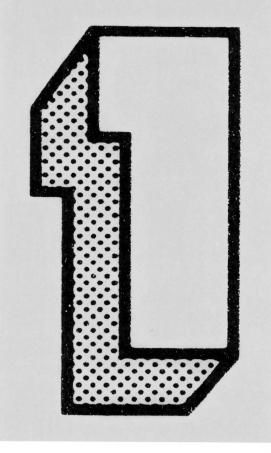

Zipper

○ ● 122

DON'T FOLLOW RULES*

* Including this one

Conformity is the opposite of creativity – as soon as you start doing as you are told and follow the rules you stop being truly creative.

Don't accept that things are always done in a certain way, find out why things are done the way they are then find out if there is a better way of doing it.

There's a lot of pressure to conform, I like it when people don't. I like oddballs (I may even be one myself). I admire individuals who do their own thing and have a unique view of the world. The interesting stuff is always on the fringes of society, never the mainstream.

Unconventional people are ingenious and inventive; it's inspiring to see the world through their eyes. It takes mavericks to show there is another way for everybody else; they are the pathfinders for new ways of living.

John Ross, the course leader of Graphic Design at Leeds Polytechnic when I was a student there, is one of these creative mavericks and he was an early influence on me ...

HELLO Mr. ROSS

My first impressions of Anthony:
A boy modelled from the Eagle comic.
He had a look that drove the shiny spaceships of my childhood.
He was very untypical, I should say. He washed and had a watch!
He had a pet rat whom he consulted on his design problems.
As far as I am aware he still keeps voles on his person.

It is well understood that the softy southern art student could
not think its way out of a wet paper bag. Each morning, Anthony
Burrill drank anthracite tea to fettle his grim-up-north bodily
brain juices. Does he still?

He would like to say that he shares 'northernness' with me,
however I come from Leicester.

John was a larger-than-life character, a painter, poet and one of the
most Northern people I have ever met. He would stride around the
college like a Victorian mill owner in hobnail boots and a wonderful
corduroy suit. He didn't take any prisoners and ran the course strictly
on his own terms. He encouraged us to push at the boundaries of
graphic design and blur the edges between disciplines.

The best piece of advice John gave me was after having a few celebratory beers at the end-of-year degree show party. He was proud that I'd successfully gained a place at the Royal College of Art to study graphic design. He put his arm around me and fixed me with a swivel-eyed gaze: 'Get down to London and fuck 'em, fuck the lot of 'em!'

Nobody thinks they are
normal or average.

We all feel we are unique and
have our own particular way of
looking at the world.

Conformity is the enemy
of creativity.

To conform is to give
up your individuality.

Your individuality is
what makes you.

You need to be yourself
to be happy.

DON'T BE NORMAL DON'T BE ORDINARY

LOOK TODAY

You are a product of your time and your environment. I graduated in the pre-digital era, probably part of the last generation of designers to be taught without using computers. Nobody I knew could afford a computer, so everything was made traditionally.

Learn to be resourceful. It's much better to use what you have around you than to spend lots of money producing something that has a limited lifespan and can't be re-used. It's about being clever with what you have and seeing the benefits in the restrictions you have.

I used lots of clip art and found images and made small photocopy publications, I was involved in the Mail Art scene, making work on the kitchen table of my girlfriend's house. It was all very lo-tech and handmade. The way the work was produced was reflected in the way it looked – very simple, minimal and bold. It's an aesthetic and an approach that I've always liked.

This is a set of pictures I made using a drawing of my studio chair. I took photographs of it then drew the simple shape. By combining it with a geometric form and playing with the elements I made a series of images that feel both abstract and playful.

LOOK
NOW
THINK
WORK
MAKE
IDEAS

MAKE NOW THINK LOOK IDEAS WORK

When I left college, I wish I had known that everything would eventually work out OK. Everyone worries about being able to make a living when they graduate, or whether a career move will work out. It's no use spending time thinking too much about what will or won't happen, the best thing to do is concentrate on making your work as good as it can be. Jump in and keep the momentum going. Do something positive every day and get your work out there. It's a boring answer and one that we've all heard lots of times before; there's no easy way or shortcut, you've got to work hard and keep going, never give up. It's difficult to talk about this stuff without resorting to cliché!

If you have a clear idea of what you want to achieve it can help guide you through those uncertain early years. Think about where you want to be and figure out a way to get there. The route is different for everyone, plus it's more exciting when you don't know what's going to happen next.

Keep asking yourself the same questions, be honest with your replies.

WHO ARE YOU WHAT DO YOU WANT?

SAY
WHAT
YOU
MEAN

MEAN WHAT YOU SAY

Never give up – you should be working to hone your approach and developing your voice at every stage of your career. Persevere and carry on knocking on doors and seeking out opportunities.

It takes time to build your confidence. Surrounding yourself with people you trust and who you can bounce ideas off is vital for that process.

PERSISTENCE IS FRUITFUL!

THIS IS WHO I AM

THIS IS WHERE I AM

Developing your strengths and learning from your weaknesses is a life-long process.

Five questions to ask yourself
when you're starting out:

What do I have to say?

How do I fit into the world?

How do I want to change the
world around me?

What is it about me that is
different from everybody else?

How important is it to me that
I make work that I'm proud of?

... And keep asking throughout your working life:

Have I been effective in communicating my opinions through my work?

Do I want to fit in or do I want to make my own way?

Have I been successful in changing things for me and the people around me?

Is it still important to me to pursue my personal goals?

Over the past twelve months have I made work that I'm proud of?

SAY YES MORE THAN NO!

For the first few years after leaving college this was my mantra, and it still is in many ways. Sometimes opportunities come along disguised as something else, you need to learn to look beyond the obvious and see how you can do somebody a good turn and also use the situation to make a great piece of work for yourself.

It's crucial to have a positive attitude, there's nothing worse than pouring cold water on somebody else's enthusiasm. Of course it's not always right to say yes, but when you're starting out it's important to jump in and get involved as much as possible. You never know who is going to see your work, where it will lead, or what the next step will be.

Never underestimate the power of positivity, it makes things happen!

I SAY YES YOU SAY YES WE SAY YES

Working in a group is a good way of finding out more about yourself. Are you a leader and an organiser or are you happy to take a back seat and be told what to do?

"NO. I MEAN YES!"

The best projects start with good conversations. In design you are communicating on many levels, so whether it is with a collaborator, client or your audience, be open, engaging and clear.

The brief that I wrote for myself at the start of my career was how to make my work relevant and communicate my personal message effectively. That has always been my personal goal. Early on, I knew I had something to say, but I was unsure about how to say it. I worked towards goals hoping things would find their own way.

Write your own brief.
Make your work relevant.
Decide how to communicate
your message effectively.
Always know what the next
stage will be.
Learn from what people you
admire have done.
Promote yourself.

THINK ABOUT ALL YOU SAY

WHAT DO YOU MEAN WHAT DOES IT MEAN?

It can be difficult to talk about your own work, especially when you're starting out, so it helps to find a way of speaking up that suits your style and that you feel comfortable with.

TELL YOUR OWN STORY

Play to your strengths and also try to work on the areas you have trouble with. Enthusiasm goes a long way.

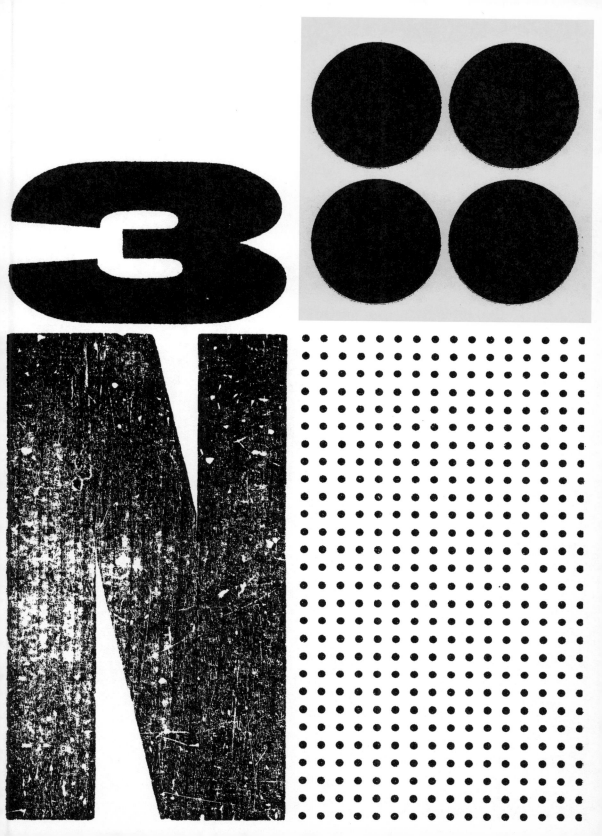

YOU & ME

Visual communication is a conversation
between two people.

Creative networks are essential, it's difficult and not much fun to work in complete isolation.

Building your creative network starts with your contemporaries, your fellow practitioners of the future. These people will form the core of your creative community, from which a rich ecosystem of creativity will develop.

By keeping those relationships alive, you give yourself a safety net and source of inspiration.

I've always sought out collaborations, it makes working life more social and enjoyable. I like the back and forth of a collaborative project, sharing ideas and working out new ways of doing things.

Working in collaboration stretches you out of your comfort zone and forces you to think quicker, taking on board other people's ideas and suggestions. Being able to let go and not try to control things too much is a good skill to develop. I like the change in dynamic from working quietly on my own to suddenly becoming part of a group. It's fun.

I WANT WHAT YOU WANT YOU WANT WHAT I WANT!

It's good to work with people who have faith in you but who also push you and encourage you to take risks. When I worked with Erik Kessels, it felt like it was the first time I was being recognised for what my work was really like. Erik has always been a big supporter and encouraged me to create work that is true to myself.

I first met Erik through Emma, when she was my girlfriend and she was shooting a campaign with him in London. He mentioned that he needed a typographer to add some headlines into the ads. She told me to go and see him with my work.

Erik sent me text for the posters; there were around twenty separate lines. In my naive enthusiasm I misunderstood his instructions and instead of picking my favourites to work on I designed all twenty posters. I worked in my usual way, photocopying the type and searching out existing pictograms that would work well with the lines of copy. He approved everything so I posted the originals to him and the posters were made directly from my handmade artwork.

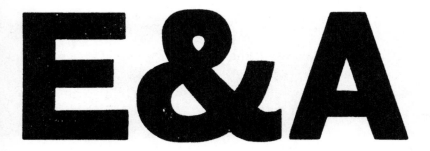

WHAT IMPRESSED YOU ABOUT ANTHONY'S WORK, WHEN YOU COMMISSIONED HIM FOR THE HANS BRINKER CAMPAIGN IN 1995?

Anthony and I had already worked together prior to the Hans Brinker campaign in 1995 so I knew he was the right guy for the job. Even at the beginning of his career, it was obvious that he'd already found his own iconic style and that he had a unique affinity with visual communication.

What impressed me from the outset about Anthony's work was the simplicity. He has the ability to strip something back to the bare minimum. A lot of people are afraid of simplicity because they think they are going to lose the message – the impact and the beauty of it. What I love about Anthony's work is that his version of simplicity enhances the message and the impact. There are not a lot of people that can do this as well as he does it. Anthony's work is simultaneously minimalistic and monumental, he only says what's necessary and that is a powerful thing.

People ask me if the Hans Brinker is as bad as it sounds. It's actually much worse.

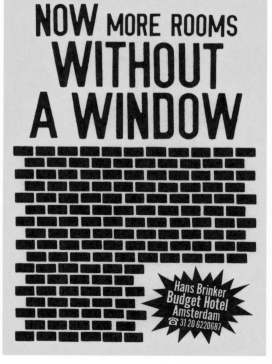

Unique Design

Hans Brinker Budget Hotel, Amsterdam
hans-brinker.com

WHAT ARE THE CHARACTERISTICS OF YOUR RELATIONSHIP WITH
ANTHONY THAT HAVE KEPT YOU WORKING SO SUCCESSFULLY
TOGETHER FOR OVER 20 YEARS?

The aspects I like about Anthony's work are the same things I like
and respect about him as a person. He's a minimalist in everything
he does. He's a man of few words, but he always picks exactly the
right ones. He's consistent, unwavering and never makes a decision
lightly. Whereas I'm intuitively expressive, spontaneous and, as a
result, a little chaotic on occasion.

I remember spending an afternoon at a funfair with Anthony, I'd
already bought a pile of stuff but he would spend ages considering
one object, analysing it from every angle, deciding where he would
put it, whether it fitted in with the rest of his interior and then,
finally… he'd put it back. Anthony and I are polar opposites and we
respect that in each other. I think that ultimately our differences
and our mutual appreciation for one another is what has formed
the basis of our friendship and our working relationship over the
last twenty years. We have totally different perspectives but we
appreciate the way the other works and this creates a dynamic that
lets us challenge each other.

Unique Design

Hans Brinker Budget Hotel, Amsterdam
hans-brinker.com

LIKE US BEFORE 👍 WE LIKE YOU!

Help us Become the Most Likeable Hotel in the World
HANS BRINKER BUDGET HOTEL

Over the years Anthony and I have become about as close as two people can get without exchanging bodily fluids. We can be completely open and honest with each other; we can say things that other people might otherwise hold back. It's rare to find someone whose opinion you respect, knowing they won't hold anything back (this can also be scary, and that's a good thing).

I think intimacy and trust is important in a creative working relationship; I'm proud of Anthony and I'm a fan of his work – still. It's always fun to work with people whose work you admire and even better if they happen to be your friend as well.

Help us Become the Most Likeable Hotel in the World
HANS BRINKER BUDGET HOTEL

MAKE IT WORK

Thinking like a designer helps in all sorts of ways, not just in choosing what colour to paint your living room. It helps you to look at a problem and decide how to solve it creatively. Don't accept that there's only one way of doing something, there are at least three. Come at a problem from an unexpected angle, turn a weakness into a strength. Don't feel that you need to conform to be successful, hold out and eventually you'll show that you were right all along.

I like the process that's involved in getting a new brief; it's always exciting to start work on a new project. I often think this is the best part of any project, the excitement that being at the beginning brings and imagining the possibilities.

The first thing to do is to find out what's required of you, the practical aspects such as timings, delivery dates and, of course, the budget. Read the brief and (with your agent, if you have one) work on the negotiations and costing a fee. Once that has been agreed, get to work on the job.

A commission from the British Library. The design is influenced by posters from the May 1968 demonstrations in Paris.

FREE SPEECH
(TICKETS £10.00)

TAKING LIBERTIES
THE STRUGGLE FOR BRITAIN'S
FREEDOMS AND RIGHTS

31st October 2008 - 1st March 2009
⊖≷King's Cross, St. Pancras and Euston
www.bl.uk/takingliberties

BRITISH LIBRARY

Commissioned by the *New York Times*, marking the anniversary of the 1963 march on Washington.

I tend to have some sort of initial briefing either in person or over the phone to outline the project. I try to ask relevant questions about the project at this point but not jump in too soon with immediate ideas and suggestions. At this stage it's important to understand what exactly is being asked of you by the client. You should appear interested and enthusiastic, but don't get carried away and start promising to deliver too much.

After the first briefing stage, start to develop your response. I like to have a good amount of thinking time, mulling things over and exploring ideas in my head before I start committing them to paper. Then bring everything together for a presentation where you can explain your thinking and how you'll approach the job. Depending on the size of the project, this might be in the form of a PDF illustrating research points, design concepts and idea developments. I usually allow a week for this initial ideas phase.

When you receive initial feedback, ideally it should be given as part of a conversation. The danger of communicating only via email is that ideas can be misinterpreted or taken too literally. It's always a good idea to speak directly about the job, to keep everything clear. You can follow up a conversation with a brief email detailing what's been agreed – this is always handy to fall back on in case of any misunderstandings.

It's always possible that there will be creative disagreements and differences of opinion. It's important to fight to keep your creative vision alive and not bend too much to please everyone. After all, they came to you to do the job, so they should trust your opinion.

Working through a job and successfully handing over the work at the end is very satisfying. Sometimes it's a relief when a job is over if it's been particularly complicated or drawn out. Occasionally it feels a bit flat when it's over, you start thinking about how the job could've worked better. But this is just the creative voice in your head that's never truly satisfied and should be gently ignored.

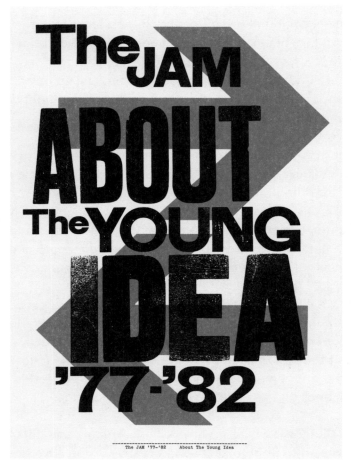

The JAM '77-'82   About The Young Idea

Commissioned by Somerset House for the exhibition 'The Jam: About the Young Idea'.

Getting the cheque is always a good bit, the first few times that happened were especially exciting. I realised I could actually make a living out of doing something I loved and enjoyed.

It takes a while to be able to look back on a project and see it objectively. When you are in the middle of a job it's hard to step back and see what you are really doing. Having a bit of time away from it gives you a new perspective.

It still gives me a kick seeing my work out in the real world. Inevitably I look for the mistakes and immediately see how I could have done things differently, but that just gives me more ideas and spurs me on to push things further on the next project.

AND YOU WHAT YOU GIVE IS WHAT YOU GET!

The JAM '77-'82   About The Young Idea

INK&
PAPER

YOU'VE ALWAYS LOOKED CLOSE TO HAND FOR WAYS TO PRINT
AND PRODUCE WORK – HOW HAS THIS SHAPED YOUR WORK?

I appear to have a special talent for seeking out printers.
I had no idea Adams of Rye existed when I moved to live near
there. The first time I saw their work was when I saw a poster
they'd printed pinned to a church noticeboard advertising a
local village fete. I could see the poster had been printed using
letterpress and typeset by someone who knew what they were
doing. I found out it had been printed by Adams and their
workshop was in Rye.

I found my local screen printer through Yellow Pages. I called
them up and knew straight away that they would be good. It's
great to find someone who is good at what they do and is willing
to experiment. I like working with people and developing a friendly
relationship, it makes life more pleasant. If I find someone who is
really good at what they do then I carry on working with them.

Adams of Rye is an inspiring place, it has an amazing atmosphere. This is something that I try to capture with the work I make there. I respond to the craft of printing, the physicality of the process and the people who work there.

WHAT IS THE PROCESS LIKE WHEN YOU WORK WITH YOUR PRINTER?

When I set type with Derek Stonham at Adams it is a collaborative
process. I go in with a rough idea of what I want to achieve, but
I always try to embrace the chance aspect of working with wood
type. Sometimes words don't fit into the layout, so I have to edit
or rewrite the phrase so it will fit. I like having this restriction
and the decisions it forces you to take.

HOW DOES THE PRINT PROCESS INSPIRE YOU?

Understanding how your work is produced is essential, it's the
only way you can experiment and move forward. I love working
with craftsmen who have amazing skills. I like to get away from
the computer as much as I can and I find working with analogue
techniques very satisfying, there's more soul in ink and paper
than there is in a microprocessor!

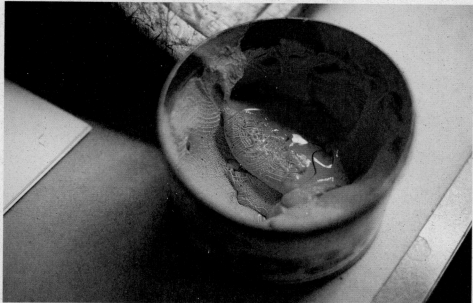

I feel a responsibility to make work of value when I'm at Adams, each print takes time to produce. I think you can see the time that has been spent when you look at the final print. Even though the finished piece is very simple, every detail has been thought about and explored.

I like the slight imperfections that come with letterpress and screen print. It's the imperfections that give the finished work its character and individuality. If something is too perfect then it loses its charm for me, I like to see the marks of manufacture and the presence of a process. I like the honesty of a handmade finish of a crafted object, I like to know that a person made it and I appreciate the time and effort taken to produce it.

By understanding how things get made you can develop new ways of approaching working. Experimenting with unfamiliar techniques makes you examine your approach, it helps you unpack your ideas. Try things that don't seem obvious, they might surprise you and lead you down a new path.

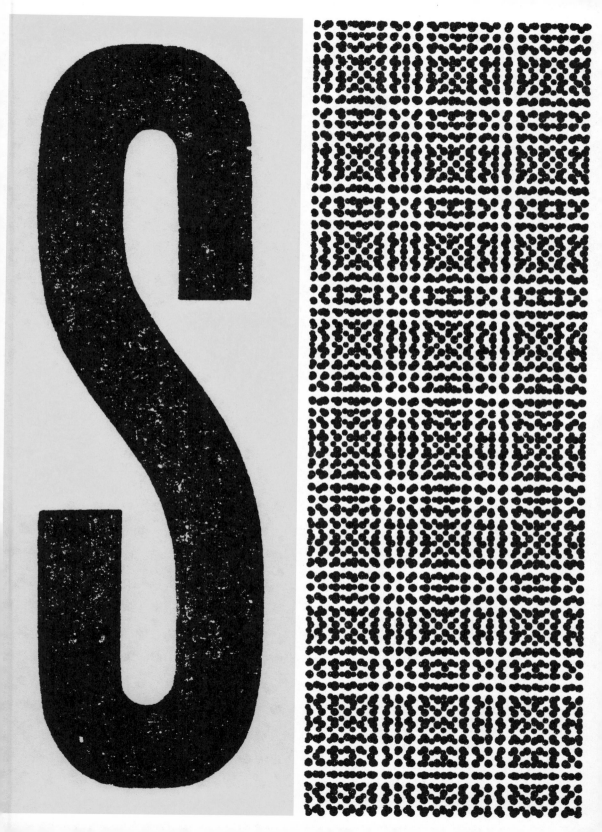

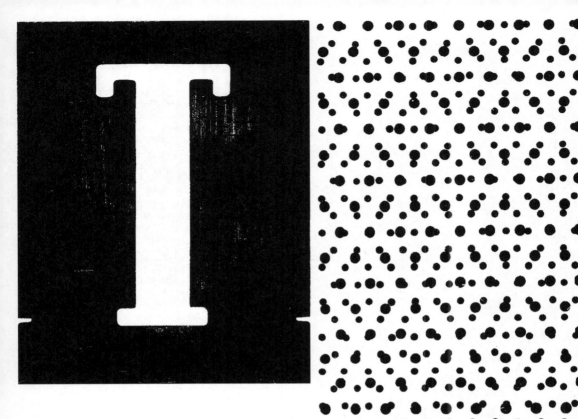

THINK & MAKE

I start work in my studio next door to the house at around 8.30 in the morning. I have various diversions and little rituals that I go through – choosing music, reading the news, tidying up and looking out of the window at the trees outside. These things might look like procrastination to the untrained eye, but this stuff is incredibly valuable. It gets me into the right frame of mind to work, it's like warming up before going for a run (I imagine).

I'm a big believer in working when it feels right and not forcing it too much. I think we only put things off that we are secretly dreading or having difficulty working out how to do. The best thing to do is just get on with it and stop diverting attention away from the job in hand. Once you get into it and start making, it will feel less of a chore and you can start to enjoy it.

Keep emails at arm's length. Email is incredibly useful but it can also become a distraction. You can't let it rule your working day. I try to check mine three times a day and have short answering sessions rather than be online all day firing emails back and forth, which can be very time wasting and break your concentration.

I'm lucky to work in a studio that's been designed specifically for me. My wife and I worked with our architects to make a space that is both practical and inspiring. The feeling of light and calm informs my work, it's a place I love working in.

I like to work on one thing at a time and try not to switch between things too much. Once I've dealt with the first batch of emails, I switch them off and get on with design work. It's important for me to completely focus on what I'm working on at that moment. I aim to work in hour-long blocks, giving myself regular breaks to get away from the computer and have a moment to think.

Letting my mind wander off at a tangent is all part of my creative process – getting bored with what I'm doing is a prompt to take a quick break and go and find something else to do. When I come back with a clearer mind I can see immediately what needs to be done. If I get too deep into something my brain gets too focused on a particular element of the design and I can't think of a way out. By having a short break it gives my brain time to think of a new way of doing things.

When a deadline is approaching it concentrates my mind and I become very focused on getting everything finished in time. I try to have extra time at the end of a project to sit with the final piece for a while. Everything benefits from having a bit more time spent looking at it and giving it a final tweak, adjusting the position of an element or changing the colour slightly can make a final design feel more considered and complete.

Reaching the end of the design process and handing over final artwork can be difficult. If I've spent a long time on a project and explored lots of different options it's tricky picking the final version to go to print. Each step in the process has its own merits. Early versions of a design possess a raw energy that gradually gets dissipated as the design is developed. It's a shame when the spontaneity is tamed by over-tweaking and this is something that I try hard to avoid.

Music is a constant in the studio – I always work best with a soundtrack to create an atmosphere.

Working late in the evening is always tempting, it's a productive time as there are less distractions. When I'm working on something I'm particularly enjoying it's hard to leave the studio. But having the discipline to choose not to work is also very important. This is part of a good work–life balance – if you aren't careful you can find yourself spending far too long at work and not enough time living your life.

I don't work at the weekend unless it's absolutely necessary to meet a tight deadline, or if a job is taking a long time to get right. Weekends can be productive as there are less weekday distractions, but it's not something that's healthy. Time away from work is valuable and should be planned for. It's when you can recharge your batteries, and getting away from the studio gives me a fresh perspective when I return.

I work best when I'm feeling calm and relaxed; I like to have time to think and reflect. Ideas need time to develop, you can't rush your natural thought process. Let ideas mature and grow at their own pace.

CLEAR YOUR HEAD

GRAFICA FIDALGA

The raw nature of the print technique is translated into beautiful texture and characterful letterforms.

In 2012 I travelled to São Paulo in Brazil to lead a workshop organised by Mesa&Cadeira, an independent education initiative. Before the trip I researched the city and came across the work of Grafica Fidalga, a traditional letterpress printers that specialised in producing street posters known as 'Lambe Lambe'. Literally translated as 'Stick Stick', this form of advertising was traditionally used across the city to promote local events. A recent city-wide ban on advertising had drastically affected Fidalga's business and it was on the verge of closing.

TRABALHE DURO & SEJA LEGAL COM AS PESSOAS

ANTHONY BURRILL PARA MESA & CADEIRA

The day I spent at Fidalga was a real test for me, I had to think on my feet, try to explain what I wanted to achieve and be resourceful. Sometimes you surprise yourself with what you are capable of.

It's important to be flexible and happy to change your plans quickly, that's something I learnt from my experience that day.

We made contact with Fidalga and arranged to spend a day setting type and printing in their workshop. I was dropped off at the print works and met Claudio, the owner. Neither of us spoke each other's language so everything was conducted using the international language of pointing and smiling.

I wanted to print a translation of WORK HARD & BE NICE TO PEOPLE in Portuguese. The phrase was hard to translate directly, the closest we got was 'Trabalhe Duro & Seja Legal Com as Pessoas' which literally means 'Work Hard & Be Cool with the People'. I love the way the translation gives the phrase a new Brazilian twist, it makes it much cooler and less English. It goes to show how collaboration can throw up unexpected but brilliant developments to your work. Claudio and I spent the day setting the type together, first choosing the letters we wanted to use, then laying them out on the bench and measuring the size once

they had been set into words. I like this way of working, it feels true to the medium and makes for interesting typography, and the result feels more like a collage than a piece of polished design.

Once we were happy with the layout Claudio set his ancient printing press to work – it rattled and groaned into life. We took an initial impression to proof the poster and it came out looking great, very raw and textured. The poster had just the right balance of slightly awkward spacing and an interesting mixture of letterforms. The wear on the wood letters gave the poster a highly textured and blocky appearance. It felt immediately Brazilian, raw and full of life.

Claudio loaded up the press with as much paper as he could find – he stacked up old printed posters intending to print on the unused side of the paper. The press lurched into action once again, but this time instead of printing another poster it ground to a halt. The drive belt connecting the machine to the electric motor had snapped, there was no way to fix it and we had to abandon printing for the day.

It was a sad and unexpected end to the day, but I brought my one poster back home and eventually made a screen-print version of it. Even when things go wrong there's something to learn from the experience and you have to keep an open mind. Although I only had one poster to show for all that effort it's given me a great story and the project got a lot of attention.

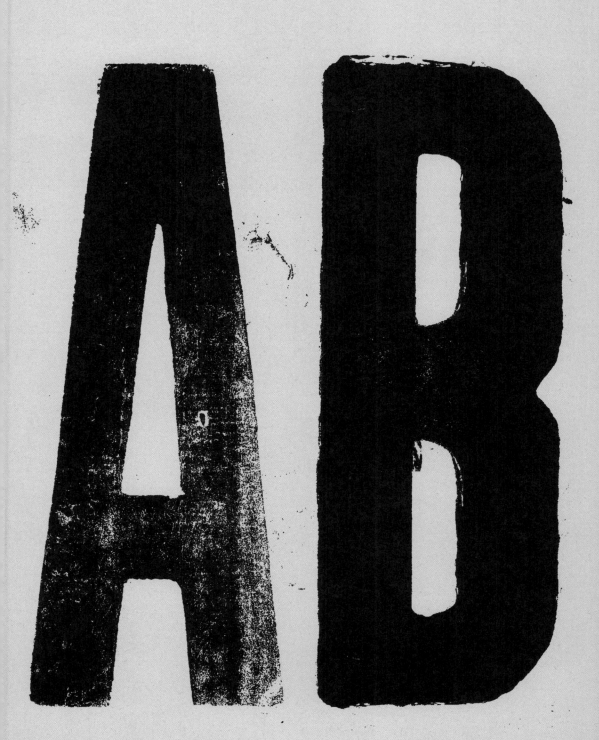

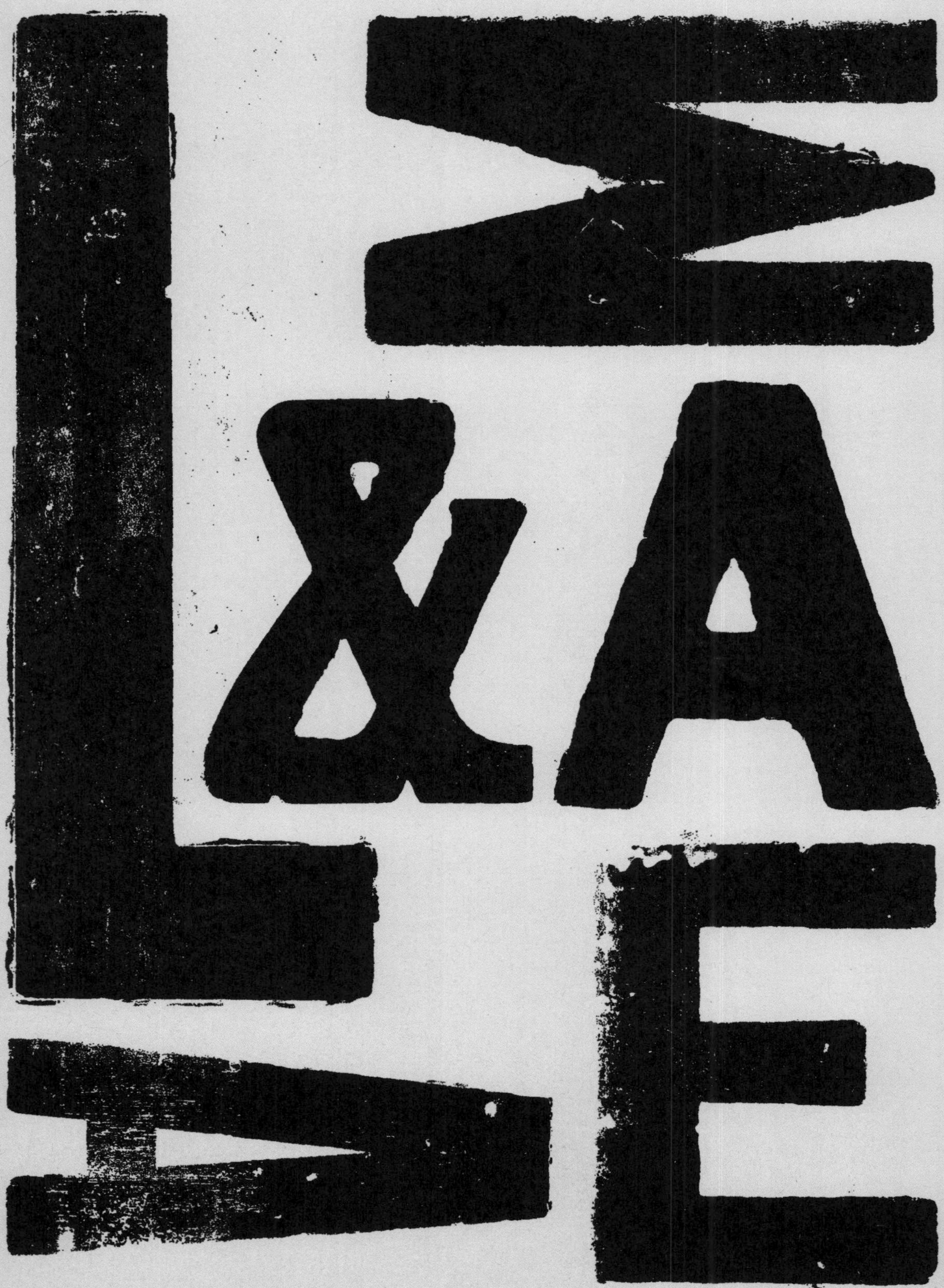
L&A
E

RS
O&GE

WANT
BETTER
NOT
MORE!

I don't need much around me in order to work, I prefer simplicity and minimum distractions.

When things are simple there is less to go wrong.

I like to strip things down to their essentials in work and life.

Think about things in a straightforward way. Try to be practical and decisive.

Simplify your life to become more productive.

Spend less energy managing chaos and have more time for reflection.

The thinking stage is the most important aspect of any project.

The best ideas can be remembered easily.

You need to know exactly what you are trying to say before you can communicate it properly.

By being brutal and cutting out unnecessary elements, your communication will be more effective.

**Don't waste time.
Be productive.**

YOU KNOW MORE THAN YOU THINK YOU DO

DO NOT NO!

HOW DO YOU APPROACH THE BLANK PAGE AT THE START OF A PROJECT?

I approach each project in a similar way, whether it's commissioned or self-initiated. My working method is straightforward: I think of all the logical steps and practical production methods that I know will work.

I tend to mull things over and work out problems subconsciously. If you give an idea a few prods and prompts, eventually potential solutions float to the surface. That way you can let problems work themselves out – don't try to overthink them. If you complicate things too much, then the first spark of an idea can become overworked and lose its spontaneity. Trust your first reaction – try hard to hang onto your initial creative impulse.

In order to fly, an idea has to feel satisfying on lots of different levels – what fonts or colours to use, how to make it, working with collaborators. All these considerations have to feel complete and 'right'.

WHAT IF YOU FEEL UNINSPIRED?

Creativity isn't a constant dependable resource, it needs to be cared for and nurtured. There's nothing worse than feeling uncreative, it can become difficult to deal with and very hard to unblock.

Giving yourself breathing space and being careful not to overwork is a good way of keeping your creativity healthy.

Sometimes the most effective way of working is not to do any work. When I'm feeling 'design fatigue' I find it hard to get excited about things that I'd normally be interested in. I take that as a sign that I need to have a break for a few days and give myself a complete rest from work. After a couple of days I find myself thinking about getting back and slowly the creative urge starts to grow again.

DON'T SAY NOTHING

ASK MORE QUESTIONS GET MORE ANSWERS!

HOW DO YOU DEAL WITH WORK STRESS?

Manage your workload carefully – it's the one thing I've learnt about staying happy. Don't take on too much and don't spend every waking hour worrying about projects. Everything always works itself out and if there is a crisis, a solution will be possible.

WHAT IF A PROJECT ISN'T GOING WELL?

Constant communication is the key to keeping things running smoothly – if you are unsure about something, ask. It's better to know what people expect of you rather than make a guess. Be clear about what you are due to deliver and when, get it done and send it in time.

HOW DO YOU DEAL WITH DIFFICULT PEOPLE?

It's part of our job as creative people; try to work through problems calmly rather than getting too emotionally involved. There is always a solution that everyone will eventually agree on, it's just a matter of explaining your decisions and demonstrating that your ideas are valid. If you feel strongly about something then you need to be able to explain why.

If I've made a decision about something that I feel is valid and it's questioned, I'll fight for it as much as I can. Explain how you reached your outcome and show that you've tried alternatives but they weren't as successful as the route you prefer. If you explain your reasoning and it's sound then it should make sense to everyone.

While it's important to stand up for yourself it's also key to be flexible. If something really isn't working, be happy to start again in a new direction. Be open to discussion and always ready to listen to input from others.

SOME SOURCES OF INSPIRATION

Design made by non-
  designers
Starting something
Kraftwerk
Photocopy machines
Friendly people
Simply designed objects
Watching a film
Eduardo Paolozzi
Looking back
Chance meetings

Vernacular type
A satisfying quality
The Human League
Fax machines
People who don't fit in
Colourful objects
Waking up early
Kurt Schwitters
Looking forward
Taking time off

Road signs
Not being too clever
Home made electronic
music
Letterpress
Helpful people
Simply made objects
Feeling challenged by
a project
DADA
Working with friends
Writing a list

Stencil typefaces
Staying in one place
Acid House Music
Self publishing
Intelligent people
Long lasting objects
Asking questions
David Hockney
New designers
Driving all day

Industrial warning signs
Keeping it simple
Casio VL Tone Keyboard
Screen print
Funny people
Beautifully simple objects
Avoiding routine
Pop Art
Long lasting friendships
Crossing off things from a list

NO ANSWER IS THE WRONG ANSWER

HOW ARE YOUR PERSONAL VALUES REPRESENTED IN YOUR WORK?

My personal values dictate and inform the work I produce. I've always been conscious that I'm continually working on a single body of work during the course of my career. Once you've been working for a few years, you begin to see patterns and themes that are repeated. I think this is positive, it shows that your impulse to produce work is coming from a single place.

WHAT IF YOU END UP HAVING TO DO WORK YOU'RE NOT HAPPY WITH?

When you're starting a new project, whether it's commercial or self-initiated, question it from every angle. Is it a project that positively represents you? Do you support the business or message that is being promoted?

Of course, it's not always that easy. I couldn't always afford to be choosy – I would gladly accept any commission that was offered. After a while I was less happy about taking on jobs that I didn't feel comfortable with. It's down to personal choice, what sort of designer do you want to be? Are you motivated solely by money or do you want to say something with your work?

There is a way of combining a personal ethos with commercial work. The two are not mutually exclusive. Develop a strong sense of who you are and work on projects you feel strongly about.

WHY SHOULD DESIGNERS ASPIRE TO AN APPROACH RATHER THAN A STYLE?

Developing a personal approach to work is essential and something that should happen to you naturally as you grow and develop. Having a distinctive approach is different from working in one style. Your personality and how you view the world should shine through your work. If your work is an honest reflection of who you are as a person then it will have longevity and stay relevant.

YES & NO NO & YES

MAKE YOUR MARK ON THE WORLD

By making work that looks fashionable and of the moment you are looking at the short term. Fashions change quickly and if your work becomes too firmly attached or associated with a particular time then your commercial career will be hard to sustain.

HOW CAN YOU KEEP EVOLVING WHEN YOU BECOME KNOWN FOR A PARTICULAR STYLE?

It's easy to be pigeonholed and put into a box that restricts your growth. Once your work has been used on a number of high-profile campaigns you become closely associated with a particular brand and that becomes part of your story.

By being careful about the type of things you work on, balancing paid projects with those that nourish you creatively, you create a body of work that sits well together and reinforces your overall message.

WAS THERE EVER A TIME WHEN YOU FELT 'LOST' CREATIVELY?

At one point I felt like I'd run out of ideas and direction. It was after a long period of working solely on commercial projects and not pursuing my own work. I had become locked into one particular way of working that was becoming routine and didn't feel exciting any longer. If that happens you have to look at how you're working and change things in your life.

A HOLIDAY FOR YOUR MIND

I made the decision to take some time off from commercial work, which gave me more time and energy to spend developing my own ideas. Selling prints from my exhibitions helped keep everything moving along while I worked out what to do next. It sounds drastic but it actually felt very natural; my first priority was to do things that made me feel happy and not feel as if work was becoming too much to deal with. It's vital that you feel happy in your work. I realised I could do something that had more value and worth, even if that meant not earning as much money in the short term.

CHANGE YOUR LIFE!

THINK OF YOUR OWN IDEAS

We can all be original.

Take your unique perspective
on the world and communicate
your own message.

Don't be afraid of doing
something different.

Stand out by being yourself and
telling your own story.

Amuse and engage people
by making characterful,
thought-provoking work.

Keep expanding and renewing
your approach.

Constantly question yourself.

Don't get bored; push yourself
and take on new challenges.

NOTHING COMES FROM NOWHERE

Questioning things is part of being creative. Everyone has pressures to be a certain way or present themselves in a certain way — your lifestyle says a lot about you, the way you dress, all that stuff. It's hard to be yourself and find out where and how you fit in. When I talk to students I try to ask them, 'What's your thing, where are you coming from, what do you want to say?' A lot of people don't have a particular message or stance, they're just trying to figure out where they fit in. It's OK. Be true to you.

WHO ARE YOU WHAT DO YOU SAY?

FIND YOUR VOICE

We are all products of our influences – I'm aware of my influences and where my visual language comes from, I understand the history of what I'm doing. You need to be aware of how you use your own personal influences and try to be inspired by ways of thinking rather than copying visual style that lacks substance.

There's a big difference between looking at someone's work and trying to understand why they make their work the way they do, and blatantly ripping off a visual style. When original work is copied or re-made with only flimsy intentions, it's bound to fail eventually. You need to have depth to your work, a personal manifesto and view of the world. Your work should come from you and not be an amalgam of whatever is fashionable at the time.

By merely taking other people's style and passing it off as your own you are being dishonest with yourself; that's not going to make you happy and it is short-sighted. There's so much going on outside of design blogs to inspire you, it's much better to look at the world around you and be inspired by that.

It takes a long time to find your own voice as a person and as a designer. It's tempting to take a shortcut to get there, but don't – you'll only make your best work and be truly happy when you are being you.

Amplify your personal view of the world,
let everyone know what you are thinking.

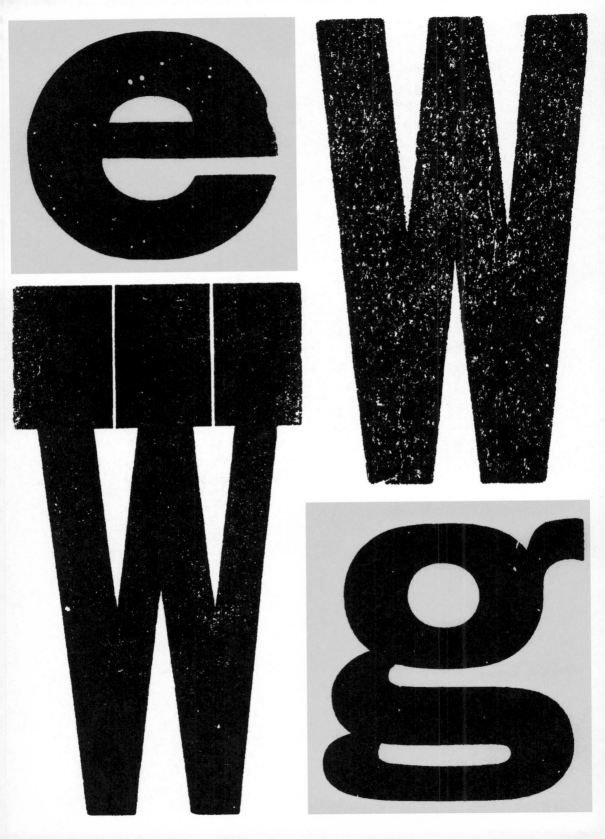

When I look at my work I see a lot of it is messages from myself to myself. Encouraging me to be braver, to believe in myself and have conviction in my ideas. When I'm being really honest with myself, that's when the best work comes out. You do your best work when you're not trying to please other people, just doing your own thing and pleasing yourself.

My work comes from a place of trying to figure things out. I don't wake up in the morning with fixed ideas, I have a rough idea of what I'm trying to achieve but the day always takes an unexpected twist or turn and I end up producing something different to what I first imagined. Sometimes the idea in my head doesn't work, maybe it's too complicated or over-stylised, that's when I start to strip things down and reduce an idea to its essence.

Of course you need to think about your audience and what you are trying to communicate, but that mustn't stop you from keeping ideas pure and individual. Good work doesn't come out of compromise. We're all frightened, that's what drives everybody — insecurity about the future. My work is a way to try to deal with that — the work is positive but it comes from a place of insecurity, not angst exactly, but a feeling of wanting to prove myself.

USE YOUR FEAR

Sometimes you can feel weighed down by previous work and sometimes it's good to forget what you've done in the past — not try to curate it too much. Just leave a trail and always be looking ahead.

I've always tried to look forwards, but sometimes when you've done a piece of work and people like it, then you want to repeat that success. When people ask you to do a job, they refer to things you've done before but you really need to have a process of creative renewal so that you're not endlessly re-making the same picture. That's a trap that illustrators can drop in to – they basically do the same picture lots of times. That's when it's good working with different collaborators, because you get a variety of influences and it sets you in another direction.

In your work you need to deal with past successes and failures — think about how you can use them to build something new.

Keep moving forward and stay relevant with your work, embrace change and create new opportunities. You can change all aspects of your work and life, don't be stifled by fear of change.

AHEAD ONLY

WE LIVE & LEARN

HAVE YOU EVER DONE A JOB JUST FOR THE MONEY?

Every designer has done work that they wouldn't admit to doing, it's a necessity to take on work that pays the bills. If you do that for too long, though, you can end up getting too dependent on commercial work and don't have enough time or energy available to do what nourishes you creatively.

WHAT'S BEEN THE TOUGHEST BUSINESS LESSON TO LEARN?

To spend less money than you make. It's easy to get carried away when you've just been paid, but when you work freelance you don't know when the next pay cheque is going to come along. It's a precarious position, especially when you take on a mortgage and start a family. Having a sense of urgency to make money to pay the bills is the strongest motivation to get your work seen by people and try to generate paid work.

HOW DO YOU GET NEW WORK?

I've always been proactive about getting my work out there and visible. If I get the feeling that work is slowing down or I'm not getting that many enquiries then I make a conscious effort to get things moving. I do this either by sending out direct mail or going to see potential contacts with my work. It's something I do less of these days, but it's never far from my mind. It's good to have a motivation to keep things moving commercially, it keeps you focused.

WHAT IS THE BEST BUSINESS DECISION YOU EVER MADE?

I think the best commercial decision I made was to start selling my prints. I first made WORK HARD & BE NICE TO PEOPLE in 2004 as a self-promotional item. The original run was of just three hundred copies, most of which I posted to friends and contacts or gave away.

Slowly I began to get requests for copies from people I didn't know, then galleries started selling them. I had to print more and it carried on growing. Eventually I added a shop section to my site and started selling directly to people. Adding more prints over time, it's been an organic process that started off as a sideline and has now grown to be a large part of what I do.

At the end of each year I give myself an 'annual review', where I take time to look at how the year has gone and the projects I've worked on, to see how I could improve or build on things that were successful. It's important to continually assess how things are going. Give yourself a push and don't get too complacent. If you stand still, you aren't pushing yourself hard enough.

Part of being creative is never feeling truly satisfied. Use this feeling to push yourself to get to the next stage of your development. There are always things you can do to improve your working methods. Look closely at how you do things, be tough on yourself.

THE
RIGHT
KIND
OF
WRONG

In 2009 the advertising agency Mother offered to host an exhibition of my work in the reception space of its London office. I'd organised exhibitions of my work in ad agencies previously, usually small displays for the creative departments, but this one was much larger in scale – the entrance space was huge, a double-height ceiling and a large open area that felt more like an industrial warehouse than an ad-agency office. I went to look at the space and realised I needed help to put on a good exhibition, it was a great opportunity and I really wanted to make a big impression.

I spoke to my friend Michael Marriott about collaborating on a custom-made display system to show some of my printed work. At first I envisaged a simple structure, something quite modest in scale and affordable to produce ...

In the end we built a four-metre-tall wooden tower on wheels, it was constructed using different types of veneer panels that were laser-cut with type and graphic devices. It featured phrases such as

RIGHT

THINK
OF
YOUR
OWN
IDEAS

'WE MUST HAVE THE TRUTH', 'RIGHT & WRONG' – all alluding to the show's theme of honesty and truth. I was feeling playful about putting such messages in the heart of an ad agency, being gently provocative and poking fun at the advertising industry (not always known for its truth and honesty). I'd had a few negative experiences while working in advertising, so I felt that this was my chance to make a comment. I'd always had good experiences with Mother – they weren't my target, it was the general perception of the advertising industry as not always being totally truthful that I was commenting on.

The Mother exhibition happened at around the same time that I decided to do less commercial work and concentrate on personal projects and cultural commissions. I'd done enough client-based work and was looking for the next chapter in my career. I wanted to work on projects that I felt strongly about, I wanted to feel like I was making a useful contribution with my work.

The exhibition was a chance for me to show what I was capable of. I'd begun to feel that I was stuck in a bit of a rut – the work I was doing in advertising wasn't fulfilling me. I needed to make a leap and push myself to make more creative work.

The exhibition went well, lots of people in the industry came to the opening. It was a big night, it felt like I'd moved on and could start to be more ambitious with my work.

Only by pushing yourself can you move forward, it's a trap to get too comfortable. It's important to use negative experiences and challenges to find a different way around things, to create opportunities. Sometimes it takes the right kind of wrong to make it right.

Working with Michael Marriott on this exhibition made me think in a new way. It was ambitious and exciting to make something new like this. The success of the exhibition spurred me on to believe more in my own work and helped give me confidence to do more of my own independent projects.

Every day something new comes along to
excite and stimulate. It's part of leading
a creative and happy life, to look and
discover. Then to turn those discoveries
into something useful that can help make
life fun and worthwhile.

A NEW IDEA EVERY DAY!

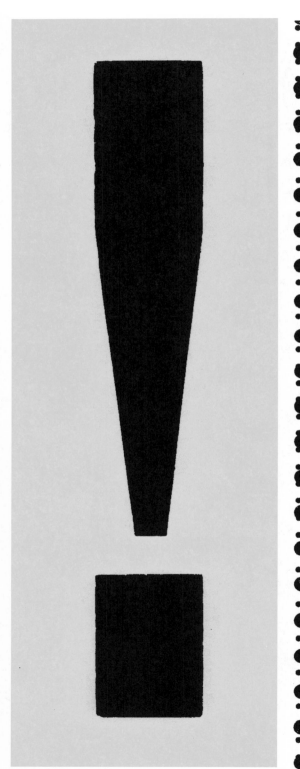
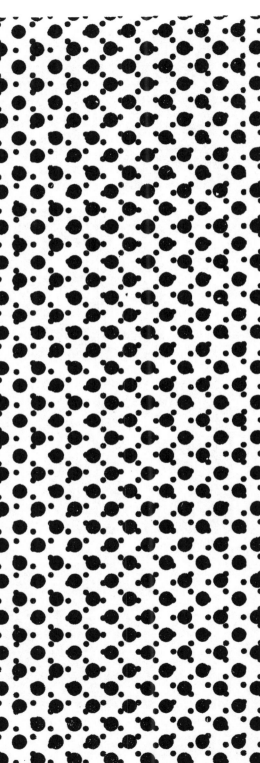

TIME TO PLAY

For a lot of people involved in creative industries, the actual work is only a small part of your development, you also need your own space to remember who you are within everything. You need to remember where that initial spark – your initial interest in creativity – came from.

School is a crucial time. You're hardwired with the urge to be creative from an early age and it can come out in different ways, whether that's through hobbies or stuff you do inside work.

You have to choose your moments when to push things a bit further. When you're doing your own work, that's the opportunity for research and development. It will influence how people see what you're about and how you approach new things.

GIVE THE JOY BACK

DESIGN FOR GOOD

Innocent Targets came through Ewoudt Boonstra, a creative I first met at KesselsKramer in Amsterdam. Ewoudt had spent time living and working in America and was shocked by the acceptance of gun culture and attitude to gun crime. Together with his creative partner Zack McDonald, Ewoudt came up with the idea of portraying the innocent victims of gun crime on a series of gun-range targets.

At first I was shocked by the campaign; it was hard-hitting but it handled the subject matter sensitively. Ewoudt asked me to help out on the design of the posters. We researched real shooting-range targets, their graphic language and how they are produced. We wanted our targets to have a convincing feel, it was important to get the details right.

It was quite scary, we'd entered a debate that was incredibly polarised and divisive. It felt right to be engaged with a subject that is so important, but I did feel nervous about the reactions we were receiving. It's important to deal with difficult subjects, to make work about something you feel strongly about. Every voice is valid, every opinion matters. You should be able to make your work about anything and help form opinions with it. As visual communicators it's our job to speak about how we see the world around us.

We made twelve posters, each using models photographed in America by Robbie Augspurger. We launched the project with an exhibition in London and tried to get as much press coverage as possible. It was picked up by broadsheet newspapers and quickly spread across social media.

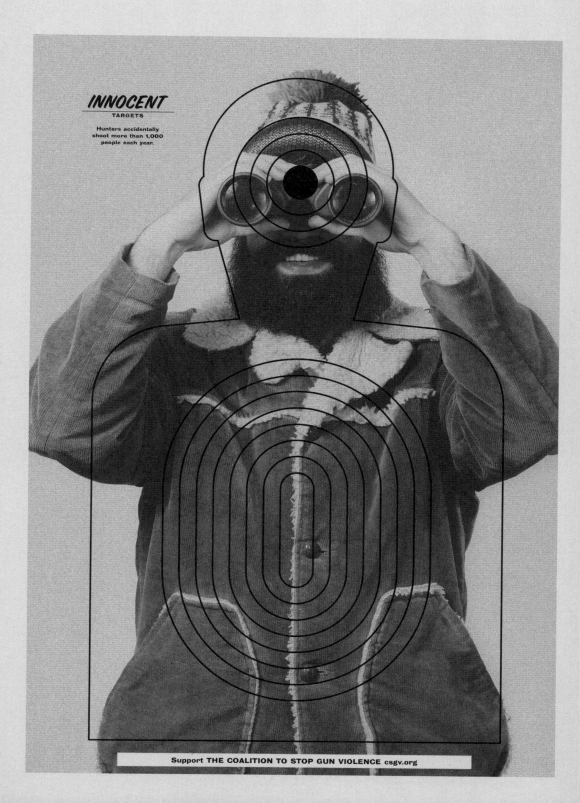

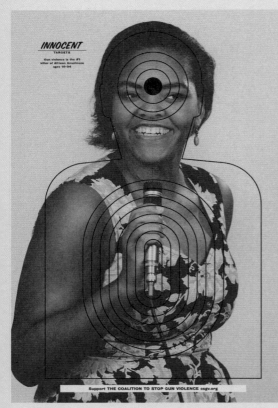

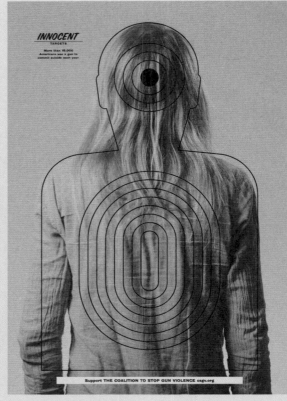

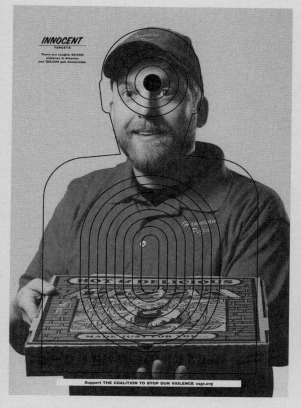

The response from Europe was positive, people were engaged and it started a debate. America was less convinced, we soon started to get very negative responses on message boards and we all received emails from the gun lobby pointing out the inaccuracies and generalisations we'd made in error. All our facts were accurate; we had a solid argument.

It was quite scary, we'd entered a debate that was incredibly polarised and divisive. It felt right to be engaged with a subject that is so important, but I did feel nervous about the reactions we were receiving. It's important to deal with difficult subjects, to make work about something you feel strongly about. Every voice is valid, every opinion matters. You should be able to make your work about anything and help form opinions with it. As visual communicators it's our job to speak about how we see the world around us.

YOU MAKE ME HAPPY

When deciding to take on a new project or to make any big decision, thinking about what makes you happy, and what doesn't, is important. These are the things that make me happy. What does your list look like?

Getting things done.

A good balance of commercial
work and self-initiated projects
happening at the same time.

The sense of satisfaction when
a project has been handed in
and approved.

A good balance between all
elements of life.

Being in control of how I spend my
time and having a creative outlet.

Ticking things off my 'to do' list.

Seeing a finished piece of work that
looks how I imagined it.

Pleasing people and getting a
positive reaction to a piece of work.

MORE SOURCES OF INSPIRATION

Hand painted lettering
Feeling happy with what
** I'm doing**
Ceefax
Cheap printing
Engaging people
Objects made from
** basic materials**
Going on a trip
Frank Stella
Old designers
Motorway service
** stations**

Worn out signs
Not being too quiet
Dial-up Internet
Mail Art
Slightly odd people
Objects made of a simple
  colour palette
Reading a book
Patrick Caulfield
Exploring a new technique
Looking at a map

Unexpected additions to
   existing signs
Finishing something
Radio
Letraset
Talented people
Easily available materials
Not knowing what is going
   to happen
Robert Rauschenberg
Taking your time
Coming home

Fragments of type
Working quietly
Philip Glass
Stencils
Challenging people
Generic objects
Finding out an answer
Jenny Holzer
Not thinking too much
The sun coming out

Hastily scrawled notes
   pinned to shop doors
Not being too busy
The college Library
Rubber stamps
Enthusiastic people
Objects that improve
   with age
Seeing an exhibition
Abstract painting of the
   1960/70s
Building on the past
Planning a trip

SPEAK UP!

This project happened as a response to the Gulf of Mexico disaster in 2010. The oil spill made headlines around the world and dominated the news. I was contacted by an agency in Brussels; they had come up with the idea to print a poster using the crude oil that had been washed up on the beaches as the printing medium.

Time was of the essence, the creatives, Tom and Cecilia, had already booked their plane tickets to fly out to America. I had to come up with a design quickly for the poster that would be printed. The first phrase I thought of was 'Oil and Water Do Not Mix'. Initially I thought this was

too simple and a bit dumb, so I carried on working on ideas, but I kept coming back to my original one. It started to sound right so I sent it over to the agency. They responded well to it, so I finalised the design and sent it over.

The next time I heard from Tom and Cecilia they were Skyping me from New Orleans. They had managed to gather the oil and were screen-printing with it. It was amazing to see it actually happening!

Once everyone was back home we set about making a site, editing a short film about the project and spreading the word. The project was swiftly taken up by social media; it was a story that could be told quickly and understood. We made a small edition of posters that were sold to help raise money for the clear up, but our main aim was to raise awareness of the disaster and keep it in the news agenda.

It's six years since the project and it still gets talked about. All the factors of 'Oil and Water Do Not Mix' came together, the basic idea was easy to grasp, the execution was done well and communicated effectively. It's easy to overthink things. Having the confidence to keep it simple, that's the difficult bit.

This is another demonstration of the power of saying yes and helping to shape a project. All the people who worked together on this did it solely to help make the project happen. We all gave our time and enthusiasm willingly because it felt right, it was a good idea simply executed.

OIL & WATER DO NOT MIX

GULF OF MEXICO - 2010

ABCDEF
GHIJKL
MNOPQ$
RSTUV★
WXYZ?-
123456
789;!&¢

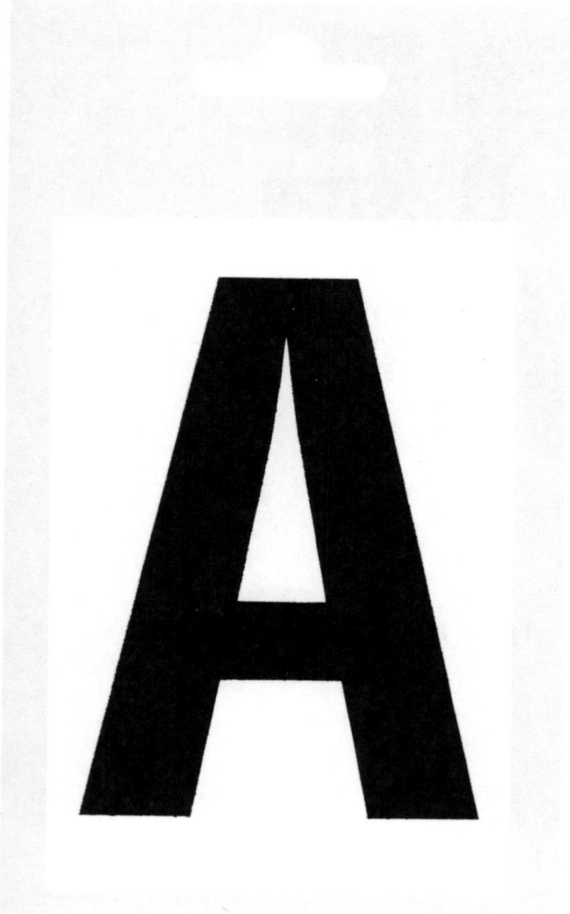
A

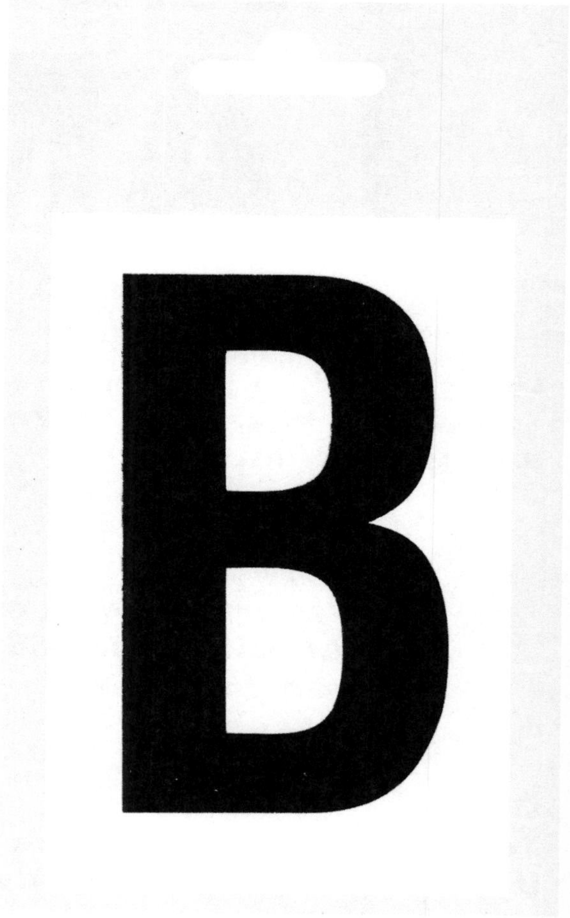
B

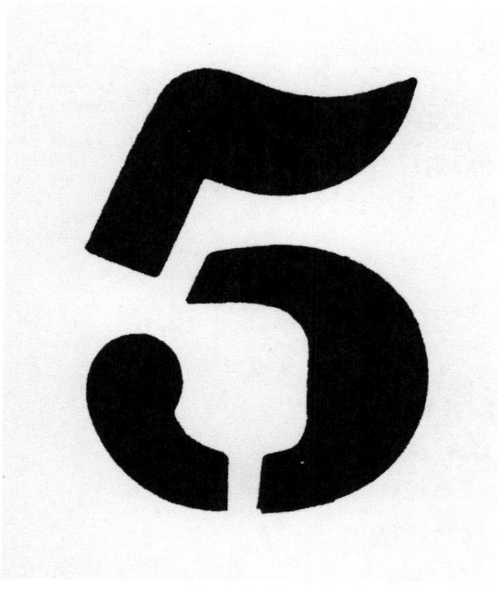
5

HERE I AM!

DO:
Talk about your work engagingly and with a touch of humour.

DON'T:
Bore everyone with overlong explanations that don't truly explain your work.

DO:
Tell a story with your work, show how it has developed. Acknowledge your shortcomings and explain how you dealt with them.

DON'T:
Be tempted to make yourself look too clever – nobody has all the answers and there are lots of different ways of doing things.

DO:
Show your human side, be honest with
yourself and the people you are talking to.

DON'T:
Speak for too long; if you can't get your
message across after twenty minutes,
then another twenty minutes isn't going
to make any difference.

DO:
Have a narrative arc to your presentation –
a beginning, a middle and an end. Reach
a conclusion, give an overview and sum up
your design philosophy. A random bunch of
projects thrown together that don't relate
to each other won't be satisfying to watch.
Think about your audience, lead them on
a journey with you.

DON'T:
Blow your own trumpet too hard, it's
important to have self-belief and a
certain amount of courage, but when
you come across as too self-important
it doesn't engage people.

DO:
Encourage questions. If nobody is willing to
ask a question, then prompt a conversation.
Read the audience and try to get a dialogue
going, it makes it more interesting for everyone.

THE WORLD IS FOR YOU!

OPTIMISM IS NOT ALWAYS DUMB

There are always two ways of
looking at a problem, from a
negative or a positive perspective.

To begin a new project is to
be optimistic.

Thinking creatively is making
a leap between imagination
and practicality.

You need to know where you are
going to feel motivated to get there.

Always be ambitious, push your
work and yourself as far as you can.

Be your own worst critic, be honest
with yourself and your work.

Optimism, energy and enthusiasm
makes everything happen.

Make work that you believe in, collaborate with like-minded people and make your own things happen. Don't rely on other people – you've got to do it for yourself.

Making a career out of doing something you love is everyone's dream. I've always done things on my own terms, I'm stubborn and focused, despite my calm, laid-back approach.

I've always felt motivated and tried as much as I can to move myself on to the next stage of life and work. My motivation has always been seeking out fulfillment; I've seen things I've wanted to achieve then gone after them tenaciously.

I love what I do and I relish the time I can spend in the studio engrossed in work. After working for twenty years I finally feel like I'm getting the hang of it.

Thanks for looking at this book, I hope you find it useful. There are no short cuts, no quick and easy ways guaranteed to work. You have to find out things for yourself. Get on and do things, whatever it is. If it's positive and done with energy and enthusiasm, it's bound to succeed!

MAKE IT NEW!

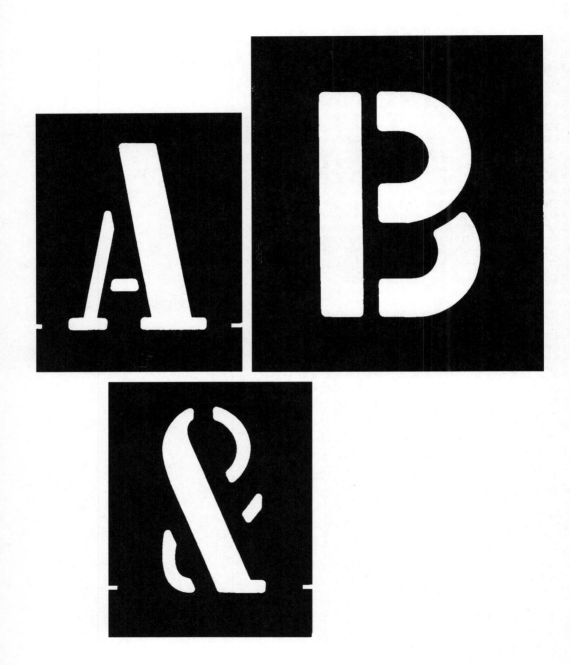

Image Credits

p.12: Human League 'Being Boiled' artwork © Holdings Ecosse Ltd t/a Fast Productions 1978; p.24–25: Stuart Hunter; p.57: Enid Michael; p.107, p.109, p.111, p.117: Cat Garcia; p.118: Jim Stephenson; p.179–181: art direction by Ewoudt Boonstra, copywriting by Zack McDonald, photography by Robbie Augspurger; p.188: © Getty Images; p.189–190: made in collaboration with Happiness Brussels, Karen Corrigan and Gregory Titeca. Art direction by Tom Galle, Cecilia Azcarate and Ramin Afshar. Photography by Tom Galle and Cecilia Azacarate.

Whilst every effort has been made to trace and acknowledge all copyright holders, we apologise should there have been any errors or omissions in this respect, and will be pleased to make the appropriate acknowledgements in future editions.

Acknowledgements

With thanks to: Elen Jones and all at Ebury Publishing, Angharad Lewis, the team at A Practice for Everyday Life, Erik Kessels, John Ross, Ian Foster and Derek Stonham at Adams of Rye, Steve Fachiri and Tracey Day at Harvey Lloyd Screen Print, Greg Burne and Alastair Coe at Big Active.

Special thanks to: Emma, Rosie and Jack Burrill.

10 9 8 7 6 5 4 3 2 1

Virgin Books, an imprint of Ebury Publishing,
20 Vauxhall Bridge Road,
London SW1V 2SA

Virgin Books is part of the Penguin Random House group of companies
whose addresses can be found at global.penguinrandomhouse.com

Copyright © Anthony Burill 2017
Anthony Burrill has asserted his right to be identified as the
author of this Work in accordance with the Copyright, Designs
and Patents Act 1988

First published by Virgin Books in 2017
www.eburypublishing.co.uk
A CIP catalogue record for this book is available from the British Library
ISBN 9780753545041

Design by A Practice for Everyday Life
Printed and bound in Italy by L.E.G.O. S.p.A

Penguin Random House is committed to a sustainable future
for our business, our readers and our planet. This book is
made from Forest Stewardship Council® certified paper.